500 Grammar Based

Conversation Questions

Larry Pitts

500 Grammar Based Conversation Questions

Copyright © 2015 ECQ Publishing

ISBN: 978-1-942116-01-1

QUICK GUIDE

ADVERBS OF FREQUENCY

We use **adverbs of frequency** to tell us how often something happens. We use them to talk about habits and how often we do things in the present or have done them in the past.

Here are some common **adverbs of frequency**:

always, never, often, sometimes, usually, seldom/rarely, ever

Adverbs of frequency come after '**be**' and other **auxiliary verbs**, but **before the main verb**.

> *He **is always** sleepy.*
>
> *She **sometimes takes** walks in the evening.*

Sometimes and **usually** can be put at the beginning of sentences.

> ***Sometimes** they watch movies late at night.*
>
> ***Usually** he gets up early.*

Adverbs of frequency questions

- How often do you read? What types of books do you like to read?

- How often do you go out to eat on weekends?

- How often do you watch TV in the evening? What shows do you like?

- How often do you eat meat for dinner?

- How often do you stay up later than you should?

- How often do you go for walks? Where do you go?

- How often do you eat fast food for lunch?

- How often do you sing? What types of music do you sing?

- How often do you listen to classical music?

- How often do you go to the movies alone?

- How often do you go to the beach in summer?

- How often do you text?

- How often do you check your email?

- How often do you check social media platforms like Facebook?

- How often do you ride a bike to work or school?

- How often do you ask your friends for help?

- How often do you skip breakfast?

AS ... AS (EQUATIVES)

We use **as ... as** to say that people or things are the same. We use **not as...as** to say that people or things are not the same.

We can use an **adjective, adverb,** or **quantifier** with **(not) as ... as.**

Adjective: *That car isn't **as** expensive **as** this car.*

Adverb: *Jack eats **as** quickly **as** Susan.*

Quantifier: *Our company doesn't have **as many** complaints **as** other companies.*

Many idioms in English use **as ... as** with an **adjective.**

*She was **as mad as** a hornet.*

*Considering that most books focus on using **(not) as ... as** with **adjectives,** the following questions have been designed to elicit this structure with adjectives.*

As ... as questions

- Are your parents as supportive as your friends?

- Are the Rolling Stones as well known as the Beatles?

- Are puzzles as fun as crosswords?

- Is modern art as beautiful as classical art?

- Is watching a play as fun as watching a movie?

- Are cats as fun as dogs?

- What's as thrilling as a roller coaster ride?

- What's as delicious as fresh baked cookies?

- Who is as important as the president of the United States?

- What travel destinations are as popular as Rome?

- Fill in the parentheses with your own idea -

- Is (city) as entertaining as (city)?

- Is (fast food restaurant) as good as (fast food restaurant)?

- Is (actor) as talented as (actor)?

- Is the (cell phone) as good as the (cell phone)?

- Is (mode of transportation) as comfortable as (mode of transportation)?

- Are (animals) as cute as (animals)?

- Is (celebrity) as strange as (celebrity)?

BE GOING TO

We form **be going to** with **present tense of be + going to + verb**. The 'be' in **be going to** is often turned into a contraction (*She's going to…*).

We use **be going to** in order to:

Talk about intentions or things we plan to do.

> *I'm going to apply to universities next month.*
>
> *The city government is going to build a new library.*

Make predictions about future events, usually when we have a reason or evidence for our predictions.

> *Don't worry. It's not going to rain. There isn't a cloud in the sky.*
>
> *He's going to win the race. Look how far ahead he is.*

Be going to questions

- What are you going to do after class?

- Where are you going to go on your next vacation?

- What are you going to do this weekend?

- How are you going to improve yourself or your life in the next three years?

- Where are you going to eat dinner tonight?

- When are you going to retire?

- What's going to be your next big purchase? When are you going to buy it?

- What show or movie are you going to watch tonight?

- What are you going to use English for in the future?

- What's going to be your next big career change?

- Who are you going to meet this weekend?

- When are you going to get up tomorrow?

- What electronic device are you going to buy next?

- Are you going to play any games today? What are you going to play?

- What piece of clothing are you going to buy next?

- What housework are you going to do this week?

- What are you going to cook this week?

COMPARATIVES

Comparatives are used to compare two things.

For one syllable adjectives: **adjective –er + than**

*He is **taller than** his cousin.*

For two or more syllable adjectives: **more + adjective + than** (to show the opposite use **less** instead of **more** before the adjective).

*This ring is **more expensive than** that one.*

For adjectives ending in 'y': **drop the 'y'** and **adjective –ier + than**

*She is **funnier than** him.*

There are exceptions – **good (better), bad (worse), far (further/farther)**, etc.

If the second person or thing being compared isn't mentioned in the sentence, we drop **than**.

*Which is **more important**, money or power? I think money is **more important**.*

We can also use **comparatives** to compare one person or thing with all the rest of the people or things in their group.

*John is **more diligent than** all of his classmates.*

Comparative questions

- Is it better to have many friends or just a few close friends?

- Compare two recent movies. Which one is more entertaining?

- Which cell phone OS do you think is better? Why?

- Which is more important, money or happiness?

- Compare two types of foreign food. Which is more delicious? Which is cheaper?

- Which is more enjoyable, going to a theme park or going to a museum? Why?

- Who is more influential, politicians or celebrities?

- Which is more relaxing, reading a book or watching TV? Why?

- Do you think that corruption or poverty is a bigger problem? Why?

- Compare two countries. Which one is a better vacation spot?

- Is it better to have more free time or more money? Why?

- Which is more important, friends or family? Why?

- Is it better to live in the country or in a city? Why?

- Compare two musicians. Who do you think is more talented?

- Which is more exciting, playing a video game or playing a sport? Why?

- Which is more comfortable, a couch or a recliner?

- Which is a better place to have a vacation, mountains or a beach? Why?

CONDITIONALS REAL WITH THE FUTURE (FIRST CONDITIONAL)

For all **conditional sentences** there are two parts, the **conditional clause** ('if' clause) and the **consequence clause** (main clause).

The **future real conditional / conditional real with the future / first conditional** is formed with **if + present simple** for the conditional clause and the **simple future will + verb** for the consequence clause. **Will** is most commonly used in the consequence clause. But **going to, must, should,** or an **imperative** can be used instead of **will.**

If I finish my homework, my teacher will be happy.

If I finish my homework (conditional clause / if clause),

my teacher will be happy (consequence clause / main clause).

The **first conditional** is used when talking about something that may happen in the future. The **consequence clause** is a realistic and possible outcome of the **conditional clause**. It is a 'real' possibility.

If you exercise, you'll be healthier.

If he doesn't study, he'll never pass the test.

The conditional clause can come first or second in a conditional sentence. If the conditional clause is first, a comma usually is put between the consequence and conditional clause. A comma usually isn't needed when the consequence clause is first.

My teacher will be happy if I finish my homework.

If I finish my homework, my teacher will be happy.

Conditionals real with the future questions

- What will you do if someone talks loudly in a movie theater while you're watching a movie?

- What will you do if you drop your phone in the toilet?

- If you go out for dinner this evening, what will you eat?

- What will you do if the power goes out in your home tonight?

- What will you do if you forget an important birthday?

- If your friend asks you to go out tomorrow evening, what will you say?

- What will you do if you crack the screen on your phone?

- What will you do if you get a raise at work or graduate from university?

- If it rains this weekend, what will you do?

- Who will you eat with if you go out to dinner this week?

- Where will go if you get an unexpected day off?

- If you meet a celebrity you admire, what will you do?

- What will countries do if the sea level keeps rising?

- What will happen if there is another financial crisis?

- If you need relationship advice, who do you call?

- What will happen if the European Union splits up?

- If humans start mining asteroids, what will happen?

CONDITIONALS REAL WITH THE PRESENT (ZERO CONDITIONAL)

For all conditional sentences there are two parts. The **conditional clause** ('if' clause) and the **consequence clause** (main clause).

The **present real conditional / conditional real with the present / zero conditional** is formed with **if + present simple tense** for the conditional and the **simple present** for the consequence clause.

> *If I forget my homework, my teacher gets angry.*
>
> > *If I forget my homework* (conditional / if clause),
> >
> > *my teacher gets angry* (consequence clause / main clause).

The **zero conditional** is used to talk about things that always happen or things that happen the same way every time. Because the situations happen they are 'real'. The **zero conditional** is used to talk about facts and behavior which don't change.

> *If I am bored, I read a book.*
>
> *If he forgets where his keys are, he asks his wife.*

The conditional clause can come first or second in a conditional sentence. If the conditional clause is first, a comma usually is put between the consequence and conditional clause. A comma usually isn't needed when the consequence clause is first.

> *My teacher gets angry if I forget my homework.*
>
> *If I forget my homework, my teacher gets angry.*

Conditionals real with the present questions

- What do you do if you're bored?

- Where do you go if you want to buy clothes?

- Who do you talk to if you have a problem?

- Where do you go if you want to read a book?

- How long does it take you to ask for help if you don't know how to do something?

- If you can't get a jar open, what do you do?

- If you go out to eat, what type of food do you eat?

- If a friend asks you for money, what do you tell them?

- If you call your parents, how long do you talk?

- If you go to the movies, do you buy popcorn and drinks? Why or why not?

- Who do you call if you're lonely?

- What do you do if you're stressed?

- If you're in a bad mood, what do you do?

- If you have a cold, what medicine do you take?

- If you want to celebrate a special occasion, where do you go or what do you do?

- Who do you talk to if you need a second opinion on something?

- What do you do if it's really hot outside?

CONDITIONALS UNREAL WITH THE PAST (THIRD CONDITIONAL)

For all **conditional sentences** there are two parts, the **conditional clause** ('if' clause) and the **consequence clause** (main clause).

The **past unreal conditional / conditional unreal with the past / third conditional** is formed with **if + past perfect** for the conditional clause, and **would have + past participle** for the consequence clause.

> *If I **had forgotten** my homework, my teacher **would have been** angry.*
>
> > *If I **had forgotten** my homework* (conditional / if clause),
> >
> > *my teacher **would have been** angry* (consequence clause / main clause).

The **third conditional** is used to talk about a past imaginary situation and the possible outcomes of that imaginary situation. In reality the situation never occurred so it is 'unreal'.

> *If I **had studied** something different in university, my life **would have been** very different.*
>
> *If you **had called** me earlier, I **would have picked** him up.*

The conditional clause can come first or second in a conditional sentence. If the conditional clause is first, a comma usually is put between the consequence and conditional clause. A comma usually isn't needed when the consequence clause is first.

> *My teacher **would have been** angry if I **had forgotten** my homework.*
>
> *If I **had forgotten** my homework, my teacher **would have** been angry.*

Would have is most commonly used in the consequence clause. But **could have, should have,** or **might have** can also be used.

If the possible outcome of the imaginary situation is in the present we use the present conditional **would + present tense.**

If I had won the lottery, I would be rich.

Conditionals unreal with the past questions

- If you had played more sports, would you have become a professional athlete?

- Did you grow up in the countryside or the city? If you had grown up in the countryside/city, would you have been more or less successful?

- If you had been born in a different country, how would your life have been different?

- If you had studied harder, would your life be any different?

- If your country's team had won the last world cup, what would you have done?

- What would you have done if you had won the last lottery?

- Where would you have moved if you hadn't moved here?

- What would you have done if you had gotten lost during your last vacation?

- What type of music would you have sung if you had been a famous singer?

- What piece of knowledge would have changed your life if you had known it?

- If you had been born a different gender, would your personality be different?

- If you had been born 100 years ago, would your life be better or worse?

- If your parents had been rich, how would your life be different now?

- If you hadn't been born in your country, what country would to want to be from?

- What language would you have studied if you hadn't studied English?

- What would be different if you had gotten different friends?

- Talk about a small decision that changed your life. What would have happened if you had made a different decision?

CONDITIONALS UNREAL WITH THE PRESENT (SECOND CONDITIONAL)

For all **conditional sentences** there are two parts, the **conditional clause** ('if' clause) and the **consequence clause** (main clause).

The **present unreal conditional / conditional unreal with the present / second conditional** is formed with **if + simple past tense** for the conditional and the present conditional **would + present tense** for the consequence clause.

> *If I **won** the lottery, I **would buy** a yacht.*
>
> > *If I **won** the lottery* (conditional / if clause),
> >
> > *I **would buy** a yacht* (consequence clause / main clause).

The **second conditional** is used to talk about imaginary situations that are not true or are unlikely. Because the situations are not true or are unlikely they are 'unreal'. The unreal conditional does not refer to the past; it refers to the present or to the future.

> *If I **had** a longer vacation, I **would travel** around Asia.*
>
> *If I **was** an animal, I **would be** a squirrel.*

The conditional clause can come first or second in a conditional sentence. If the conditional clause is first, a comma usually is put between the consequence and conditional clause. A comma usually isn't needed when the consequence clause is first.

> *I **would buy** a yacht **if** I **won** the lottery.*
>
> *If I **won** the lottery, I **would buy** a yacht.*

Conditionals unreal with the present questions

- What would you do if you were elected the leader of your country?

- What would you tell yourself if you could go back in time and talk to your younger self?

- If you could create a superhero, what would their power and name be?

- What would you do if you were the second richest person in the world?

- Who would you marry if you could marry anyone in the world?

- If you could take one thing from the past and bring it to the present, what would it be?

- If you were able to change places with one person for one day, who would the person be? What would you do?

- If you could choose to live forever, would you?

- If you were an animal, what animal would you be?

- If you had only one week to live, what would you do?

- What year would you travel to if you had a time machine?

- If you could meet any three people from any time or place who would you meet?

- What spell would you want to know if you were a wizard?

- If you could have any animal as a pet, what animal would you want?

- If you were famous, what would you be famous for?

- If you could be a master at one skill, what would you be a master of?

- What would you want if you could eat anything right now?

FOR, SINCE

We use the preposition **for** to say how long something occurs. We use the preposition **since** to say when something started.

*They have been waiting in line **for** 2 hours.*

*They have been waiting in line **since** 1pm.*

*He has worked in this restaurant **for** 5 weeks.*

*He has worked in this restaurant **since** November.*

Since can only be used with **perfect tenses** (past perfect, present perfect continuous, etc.). But **for** can be used with **all tenses**.

*He **worked** on his homework **for** three hours.*

*She **will jog for** 2 hours tonight.*

*He **has been working since** 7pm.*

For, since questions

- What's your most prized possession? How long have you had it?

- Do you play a sport? How long have you played it?

- How long have you been a fan of your favorite singer or group?

- What's the longest time you've slept?

- How long have you had your watch?

- What's the longest amount of time you've spent alone?

- How long have you had your phone?

- How long have you been awake today?

- How long has your country been a country?

- How long have you been a student here?

- What's one of your hobbies? How long have you been doing it?

- What piece of clothing have you had the longest? How long have you had it?

- How long have you had your shoes?

- How long has the leader of your country been in power?

- How long have you had your TV?

- Who is your favorite sports team? How long have you been a fan?

- What's your favorite restaurant? How long has it been open? How long have you been going to it?

GERUNDS VS. INFINITIVES

A **gerund** is a **verb ending with –ing** that functions like a noun. **Gerunds** can be used as subjects, direct objects, subject complements, and as objects of a preposition.

Running is fun. (Gerund as subject)

*I love **running**.* (Gerund as direct object)

*I never gave **running** a thought.* (Gerund as indirect object)

*Do you object to **running**?* (Gerund as object of preposition)

We often use **to + infinitive** after certain verbs, especially thinking and feeling verbs. They have lots of other uses including being used to show purpose, after certain adjectives, to give opinions and more.

We'll focus on **gerunds** and **infinitives** being used after certain verbs because most books compare gerunds and infinitives in this way. Just keep in mind that **gerunds** can be used in other places instead of nouns and **infinitives** have other uses as well.

When **gerunds** are used after a verb, they can only follow certain verbs. Other verbs need the **infinitive (to + verb)**. Still other verbs can use both **gerunds** and **infinitives**.

*I enjoy **walking**.* (enjoy = **gerunds not infinitives**)

*He attempted **to run**.* (attempt = **infinitives not gerunds**)

*She hates **running**.* (hate = **gerund or infinitives**)

*She hates **to run**.*

Some verbs such as **stop, remember, forget,** and **try** change meaning depending on whether a **gerund** or **infinitive** is used.

Some verbs can take a **direct object and an infinitive.** The structure looks like: **verb + direct object + to + infinitive.**

> *She **invited me to go** to the dance.*

We can use **make, let,** and **help** with the above structure but without the 'to'.

> *He **helped me finish** my homework.*

Not every verb ending in -**ing** is a **gerund**. A verb ending with −**ing** can also be a **present participle**.

*The **following questions** attempt to elicit **gerunds**. The verbs used in the questions can take gerunds but not infinitives as direct objects.*

*The **next set of questions** after the gerunds attempts to elicit only **infinitives**. The verbs used in those questions can take infinitives but not gerunds.*

Gerund questions

- What's something you avoid doing?

- Is there something you're considering doing? What is it?

- What are some activities you dislike?

- What type of exercise do you hate?

- What kinds of activities does your job or studies involve?

- What housework do you not mind doing?

- Is there anything you keep doing even though you know you shouldn't?

- What are some high school activities you miss doing?

- What activities do you recommend to stay healthy?

- What's an activity you practice every week?

- Do you think that playing games is a worthwhile activity? Why or why not?

- What do you enjoy doing on the weekend?

- What do you delay doing until the last minute?

- What are some habits you dislike?

- What's something you keep thinking about doing but haven't?

- What do you plan on doing after class?

- What do you always complain about doing?

Infinitive questions

- What's some work you choose to do even though you don't have to do it?

- What's something you hope to do in the future?

- What's something you always forget to do?

- What do you want to do after class?

- What do you tend to do when you're sad?

- What's something you tried to do but failed at?

- Is there anything you refuse to eat?

- Where do you plan to go on your next vacation?

- Have you ever vowed to do something?

- Is there anything you're striving to do?

- Where are some places you want to go on vacation?

- Do you ever pretend to work? Why?

- What do you tend to do when it's raining?

- What's something you're yearning to do?

- What do you want to do this weekend?

- What are some crazy things you've tried to do?

- What's the next big project you plan to do?

- What are some things you're glad you agreed to do?

IMPERATIVES

Imperatives are used to tell someone to do something or how to do something. To make an **imperative, drop the subject** and **use the base form of the verb**.

Add four cups of flour.

Don't sit on the couch all day.

Imperatives are used:

To give instructions.

To give orders.

Click the green button.

Stop running around and come here!

To give advice or a suggestion.

To offer something.

Find a job you love.

Have a cup of coffee.

You can use signal words like **first, next, then, after that,** etc. to show order when using **imperatives**. Signal words serve to guide the listener/reader from one idea to the next.

First, dice the onions. Then, fry the chicken.

Imperative questions

- Tell me how to make some kind of delicious food.

- What should someone do if there is an earthquake?

- How do I get to a good restaurant near here?

- What are your best tips for a happy marriage?

- Tell me step by step how to make a lot of money.

- What should I do if I see someone who is cut very badly?

- What's a card game from your country? How do I play it?

- How does a person find the perfect man or woman?

- What are your best tips to live a happy life?

- How do I get to the nearest bus stop?

- Can you give some tips for surviving a flood?

- What should I do if there is a flood?

- Tell me some tips for a hobby you have.

- What should I do if I'm in a car accident?

- Tell me how to plan a great vacation.

- Can you tell me how to do a traditional dance from your country?

- What should someone do to escape a burning building?

MODALS OF ADVICE
(should, ought to, had better)

We use **modals of advice** to give advice and say what we think is a good or bad idea.

We form modals like this: **modal + verb** (base form). The 'to' in **ought to** is considered part of the modal.

Should is the most common modal of advice. It can be used with questions, negative sentences, and affirmative sentences.

> *Where **should** I **park**?*
>
> ***Should** I **exercise** more?*
>
> *You **shouldn't drink** that milk.*
>
> *You **should bring** an umbrella.*

Had better is the strongest modal of advice. It implies that if you don't follow the advice, something bad will happen. It can be used with negative and affirmative sentences.

> *She **had better not be** late again.*
>
> *They **had better** slow down.*

Ought to is the least common modal of advice. It can only be used with affirmative sentences.

> *He **ought to start** jogging.*

Modals of advice questions
(should, ought to, had better)

- Where should I go on my next vacation?

- What should a person look for when dating?

- Should a husband and wife share household chores? Why or why not?

- What are some things a person ought to do to get a good job?

- What are two things a person ought to do to have a happy life?

- What are some things a person had better or had better not do during a job interview?

- What are some things I'd better not do if I want to live a long time?

- Who are some musicians or bands I ought to listen to?

- Where should I go to buy electronics?

- Should the work week be four days instead of five? Why or why not?

- What's something every person should do before they die?

- What are two things a person ought to do if they visit your country?

- Are there any things a tourist had better not do if they visit your country?

- How old should a person be before they can buy cigarettes? How about alcohol?

- What are some things parents had better teach their children?

- What's something that isn't a law but should be?

- What's one thing everyone ought to study?

- What are some things I'd better do when traveling abroad?

MODALS OF NECESSITY
(must, have to, have got to)

Modals of necessity are used to show that something is necessary.

We use modals together with main verbs: **modal + verb** (base form). With **have to** and **have got to** the '**to**' is considered part of the modal.

Must is the strongest modal of necessity. It is most often used in writing. It is not commonly used in questions.

> *They **must check** their bags before boarding the plane.*
>
> *You **must not smoke** here.*

Have to is the most commonly used modal of necessity. It can be used for questions. **Have** (**have / has**) changes form depending on the subject in affirmative sentences. **Do** is necessary for questions and negative sentences.

> *He **has to go** to work tomorrow.*
>
> *They **have to leave** early on Sunday.*
>
> *She **doesn't have to stay** late.*
>
> *Do you **have to get** a new phone soon?*

Have got to is used most often in informal speech. It cannot be used for questions. It is not commonly used in negative sentences. **Have** changes form depending on the subject in affirmative sentences.

*We **have got to get** a new refrigerator.*

*He **has got to buy** some new clothes.*

We only use **had to** when talking about the past. We don't use **have got to** or **must** to talk about the past. When talking about the past **have to** becomes **had to**.

*He **had to work** all night last night to finish the project.*

Modals of necessity questions
(must, have to, have got to)

- What are some things you have to do when you get home?

- What are some things you must do or must not do when you go to the airport?

- What do students have to do if they want to improve their English?

- What are some unusual or harsh laws in your country?

- Which types of workers have to work the hardest?

- What are some things you must or must not do at your job or university?

- Is there anywhere you have to go after class?

- What does a person have to do to become successful?

- What are some things you have to do but don't want to?

- What must a person do to be happy?

- Who is someone you must listen to?

- What are some interesting customs in your country that people have to follow?

- Where must you go even though you don't want to?

- How many hours of sleep do you have to get to function normally?

- Is there anything that you have to eat at least once a week?

- What are two things your parents said you must do?

- What are some things all humans have to work together to accomplish?

MODALS OF POSSIBILITY AND PROBABILITY
(may, might, could, must, can't)

We use modal verbs in combination with main verbs: **modal + verb** (base form).

Must is used to show that we are certain.

> *Wow, you are really sweaty. It **must be** hot outside.*

Can't is used to show something is impossible.

> *We **can't give** him the job because he doesn't have enough experience.*

May, **might**, and **could** are used to talk about present or future possibilities. They can be used to explore possible options for the future, to make suggestions in order to solve a problem, or to guess about a situation when we don't have all the facts.

> *After I finish university I **may go** abroad or I **may try** to get a job right away.*
>
> *Your car **might be** having problems because the battery is too old.*
>
> *The remote control **could be** in the couch.*

May not and **might not** can be used to show that present or future possibilities are not likely. But **could not** cannot be used in this way.

> *He **may not graduate** if his grades don't improve.*
>
> *They **might not go** on vacation this year.*

Modals of possibility and probability questions
(may, might, could, must, can't)

- What are some things you may do this evening?

- What are three good things that may happen soon in your life?

- Is there anything you can't do even though you want to?

- What movie might win the Academy Award for best picture this year?

- Is there anything that could make you change your major or quit your job?

- Where might you be living in 5 years?

- What are two things that could make you much happier?

- What are some goals you might accomplish in the future?

- In what ways do you think your country may improve in the future?

- What are three things all humans must learn to do better?

- What are some problems the world might face in the future?

- What are some things that could improve the economy in your country?

- For the following questions, talk about how certain you are of your opinion using modals -

- Do you think that aliens exist? Why or why not?

- Do you think that people are born good, evil, or neutral? Why?

- Talk about some conspiracies you've heard. Do you believe them or not?

- Do you think that most politicians start their careers with good intentions?

- What do you think made people stop hunting and gathering, and start farming?

NOUNS (COUNT / NONCOUNT)

Count (countable) nouns can be counted or numbered. Count nouns have singular and plural forms.

Noncount (uncountable) nouns cannot be counted or numbered and they do not have a plural form.

We can use a/an and the with singular count nouns. We can use the and many with plural count nouns.

> *Do you have **a pencil** I can borrow?*
>
> *I would like **an apple**.*
>
> *He opened **the window**.*
>
> *She watered **the plants**.*
>
> *The farm had **many pigs**.*

We can use much and the with noncount nouns. Much is usually only used in questions and negative statements. Much is rarely used with affirmative statements.

> *He doesn't have **much money**.*
>
> ***The mail** arrived an hour ago.*

We can use some, any, no, and a lot of / lots of with both count and plural noncount nouns. Any is usually only used in questions and negative statements. Any is rarely used with affirmative statements.

> *Would you like **some strawberries**?*
>
> *No, but I would love **some juice**.*

*Sorry, but we don't have **any juice**.*

*I suppose you have **no milk** either.*

*Actually, we have **a lot of milk**.*

*So you have **lots of milk** and **a lot of strawberries**?*

Yes.

*Do you have **any blueberries**?*

*Yes, we have **lots of blueberries**.*

*Then I'll have a strawberry and blueberry **smoothie**.*

Some nouns are **count** and **noncount** nouns with different meanings depending on whether they are **count** or **noncount**.

*The **woods** are beautiful this time of year.*

*This house is made of **wood**.*

Most **noncount** nouns can have a countable container included to make them act more like count nouns. Usually '**of**' is added after the container.

*Can you get me some **milk**?*

*Can you get me three **cartons of milk**?*

In informal language sometimes the container is dropped from the sentence and the **noncount** noun is used as a **count noun**. This is often done when talking about food or drinks.

*We'll have **two cups of coffee**.*

*I'll have **two coffees**.* (We mean two cups of coffee.)

Noun (count / noncount) questions

- How much water do you drink in a day?

- What kinds of food do you eat regularly?

- What did you order last time you went to a restaurant?

- Do you eat any special foods on New Year's Day? If so, what do you eat?

- What are some of your favorite types of vegetables?

- What's your favorite type of meat? Why is it better than other types?

- What would you like to grow if you had a garden?

- What types of ingredients go into your favorite dish?

- What are some unhealthy foods that you love?

- What spices do you use most when you cook?

- What do you usually order when you go to your favorite fast food restaurant?

- What do you eat when you go to watch a movie?

- Do you prefer eating utensils made from wood, metal, or plastic?

- What's your favorite fruit? How much do you usually eat in one sitting?

- What drink do you like to have with meals?

- What kind of condiments do you use a lot? What types of food do you put them on?

- What do you eat when it's cold outside?

PASSIVE VOICE IN THE PRESENT (PRESENT PASSIVE VOICE)

Passives are formed when the agent (doer of the verb, the noun phrase found in the subject position in active sentences) switches places with the patient (the receiver of the action of the verb, in the object position in active sentences).

We make **the passive voice in the present** (present passive voice) with the **present tense of be+ past participle of the main verb**. The form of *be*-verb changes depending on the subject.

We use **the passive voice in the present:**

When the person or thing (agent) that did the action isn't known or isn't important.

> *The best cars **are made** in Germany.*

To talk about processes.

> *First, the rock **is pulverized** to produce a powder.*
>
> *Next, the powder **is compressed** into a 5 cm thick sheet.*

To sound impersonal in formal writing (e.g. news reports, scientific papers, etc.).

> *Interesting conclusions can **be drawn** from these findings.*

When we want to show who or what did the action we use **by.**

> *This brand of wine is made **by** well paid workers.*

Passive voice in the present questions

- Where are the best suits made?

- Who are the best cell phones made by?

- Where are the worst cars made?

- Where is most of the world's oil extracted?

- What is the process to make a great wine?

- Where are the best football players born?

- Where are most technical advances made?

- Where are the best watches made?

- Who are the best TVs made by?

- What do you know the process for making? What are the steps for making it?

- In what country is football played most?

- Who are the best films directed by?

- Where are most computers made?

- Who are the best shoes made by?

- Who are the best cars made by?

- What sports are played most in your country?

- Where is the best tea grown?

- Where are the best games created?

PASSIVE VOICE WITH THE PAST

Passives are formed when the agent (doer of the verb, the noun phrase found in the subject position in active sentences) switches places with the patient (the receiver of the action of the verb, in the object position in active sentences). We make the **passive voice with the past** (past passive voice) with the **past tense of be + past participle**. The form of 'be' changes depending on the subject.

We use the **passive voice**:

When the person or thing (agent) that did the action isn't known or isn't important.

> *The most beautiful paintings **were made** during the Renaissance.*
>
> *My wallet **was stolen**!*

To talk about processes.

> *The sugar **was added** and then **heated** to 250 degrees Celsius.*
>
> *The mixture **was** then **stirred** for 10 minutes.*

To sound impersonal in formal writing (e.g. news reports, scientific papers, etc.).

> *The town **was destroyed** in a tragic twist of fate.*
>
> *Blame **was laid** on the politicians involved.*

When we want to show who or what did the action we use '**by**'.

> *His sandwich **was stolen by** a squirrel.*

Passive voice with the past questions

- Who were your clothes made by?

- Have you ever had anything stolen from you?

- Who was your phone made by?

- Who were your shoes made by?

- Where were you born? Were you raised there, too?

- What's your favorite book? Who was it written by?

- What's your favorite song? Who was it sung by?

- What's your favorite movie? Who was it directed by?

- Talk about when you were given bad service at a restaurant.

- Where were you first exposed to English?

- Who was your favorite game made by?

- Who were the best plays written by?

- Who were the greatest symphonies composed by?

- In what country were the greatest works of art created?

- What's the greatest invention? Who was it invented by? Where was it invented?

- What's the most important building in your country's history? Who was it built by? When was it built?

- What is the most mysterious monument from your country's history? What do you think it was used for? When was it made?

PAST CONTINUOUS

We form the **past continuous** with the **past tense of be + verb with -ing**.

We use the **past continuous** to:

Talk about a situation or action that continued for a period of time in the past and was completed in the past.

> *The workers **were repairing** the roads last week.*
>
> *My stomach **was hurting** after I ate that burrito.*

Talk about two actions that were both happening at the same time in the past.

> *My roommate **was talking** on the phone while I **was watching** a movie.*
>
> *The roofers **were working** on the roof while we **were painting** the walls.*

Talk about an action that happened before, during, and after a certain time.

> *I **was sleeping** last night at 12am.*
>
> *She **was driving** home at 7:30pm last night.*

Talk about an action that was completed repeatedly in the past, but does not occur any longer.

> *He **was smoking** three packs a day.*
>
> *They **were having** meetings 3 times a day.*

Past continuous questions

- What were you doing yesterday at 3pm?

- What were your friends doing Saturday evening?

- What were you doing right before class?

- Who were you talking to yesterday afternoon?

- What were you eating the last time you spilled food on your clothes?

- What were you doing Friday night at 9pm?

- What were you doing last New Year's Eve at 11:30pm?

- Were you watching a movie last Sunday at 8pm?

- Who were you texting before class?

- What were you doing yesterday at nine in the morning?

- What TV show were you watching Monday night?

- What were you doing the last time you got a phone call?

- Were you working hard last night? What were you doing?

- What were you doing last Christmas morning at 10am?

- What were you doing the last time you got caught in the rain?

- What were you doing while you were eating dinner last night?

- What were you doing the last time someone told you to stop being childish?

PRESENT PERFECT

We make the **present perfect** with the auxiliary verb **have/ has** and the **past participle of the main verb**. The form of **have (have / has)** depends on the subject.

*I **have eaten** at this restaurant many times. / She **has been** to Spain.*

*We **haven't started** yet. / He **hasn't read** that book.*

*Where **have** you **been**? / What **has** she **made** in art class this week?*

***Have** you **tried** this before? / **Has** he **worked** here for long?*

We use the **present perfect** to:

Talk about something that started in the past and continues into the present.

*We **have lived** in this apartment since April. (They moved into the apartment in April and are still living there now.)*

Talk about an action that has been completed multiple times in the past.

*Peter loves that movie. He **has seen** it 16 times since last year.*

Talk about what has or hasn't happened up to the present. Add **never** to make a negative statement, and use **ever** when forming yes/no questions.

*John and Sarah **have never been** to Egypt.*

***Have** they **ever** been to Korea?*

Talk about something that happened in the past and is important or relevant to the present moment.

*Jane **has seen** that movie. Let's watch a different one.* (It's important that Jane has seen the movie because the group is deciding what movie to watch.)

Present perfect questions

- Where are some places you've been on vacation?

- What are some strange types of food you've eaten?

- How many times have you been to a theme park? Which ones have you been to?

- What different countries have you traveled to?

- What are some good restaurants you've eaten at?

- What's something you've done that you're very proud of?

- What interesting hobbies have you tried?

- What are some wild things (e.g. bungee jumping) you've tried?

- What's something you've started but haven't finished yet?

- Have you tried Thai or Turkish food? What other international cuisine have you tried?

- What are some hobbies you've tried?

- Have you broken any bones? Which ones have you broken? What happened?

- Where are some interesting places you've been in your country?

- What animals have you ridden?

- Have you ever been camping? Where have you camped?

- Have you ever gone fishing? What types of fish have you caught?

- Who have you met that is famous or slightly famous?

PRESENT PERFECT CONTINUOUS

We form the **present perfect continuous** with **have / has been + verb -ing**.

We use the **present perfect continuous** to:

Talk about the duration of an action that was started in the past and is still happening now. Often "for" or "since" are used.

> *This company **has been making** furniture since 1952.* (The company is still making furniture.)
>
> *I **have been feeling** sick all day.* (I still feel sick.)

Talk about an action that was started in the past and just recently finished.

> *She **has been working** all day but she finally finished.*
>
> *I **have been reading** this book for three hours; I should take a break.*

Talk about a series of repeated actions happening from the past to the present.

> *John **has been checking** his mail box every hour or so.*
>
> *We **have been playing** soccer here every Saturday for three years.*

Present perfect continuous questions

- What's a project you've been working on for a while?

- Have you been eating healthy or unhealthy food recently?

- What have you been doing to improve yourself this year?

- What music have you been listening to recently?

- Who have you been hanging out with a lot this month and last month?

- Where have you been going a lot this month?

- How long have you been attending this school?

- Have you been exercising this month and last month?

- What have you been doing in your spare time this week?

- What sports teams have you been following recently?

- Have you been trying anything new recently?

- Who have you been talking with the last few days?

- Where have you been going a lot in the past couple of weeks?

- Have you been getting enough sleep?

- What game have you been playing a lot recently?

- Are there any news stories you've been following?

- What have you been thinking about buying?

QUANTIFIERS

Quantifiers are used to give information about quantity (**how much** or **how many**).

You can use a **noun after a quantifier** when you are talking about things in a **group in general**.

Most restaurants are clean.

Many fish contain mercury.

To talk about a **specific group** use '**of the**'.

Most of the restaurants in this neighborhood are clean.

Many of the fish in this lake contain mercury.

These **quantifiers** can be used with **count** or **noncount** nouns.

all	*a lot of*	*no/none*
any	*lots of*	*none of*
enough	*more*	*some*
less	*most*	

These **quantifiers** can only be used with **count nouns**.

many	*(a) few / fewer*	*a great number of*
both	*neither*	*a couple of*
each	*several*	
either	*a large number of*	

These **quantifiers** can only be used with **noncount nouns**.

a little	*a bit of*	*a large amount of*
(not) much	*a great deal of*	*a large quantity of*

Quantifier questions

- How much fruit do you eat in a week?

- How many times do you go to the movies in a month?

- How many phone calls have you made this week?

- How much of a pizza do you eat during one meal?

- How many games have you downloaded on your phone?

- Do any members of your family smoke? How many cigarettes do they smoke in a day?

- How many songs do you have on your phone?

- How many DVDs do you have at home? How about VHS tapes?

- How many vinyl records do you have at home?

- How much time do you spend on your phone every day?

- How much water do you drink in a day?

- How much money do you spend on going out to eat every week?

- How much soda do you drink in a week?

- How many pets have you owned?

- How many hours do you spend playing games every week?

- How much money do you spend on vacations every year?

- How much foreign food do you eat?

REPORTED SPEECH / INDIRECT SPEECH

We use **reported speech** (indirect speech) to talk about what people said or asked. When moving from **direct speech** (*"I am tired."*) to **reported speech** (*He said he was tired.*) the verbs, pronouns, and word order usually change. When reporting normal direct speech we usually use **say** or **tell**. When reporting questions, requests, orders, and advice we use other words.

Direct speech: simple present

"*I like ice cream.*"

Reported speech: past tense

He said he **liked** ice cream.

If what was said in the direct speech is still true, the verb can stay as the simple present in reported speech.

"*I eat lunch at 1pm every day.*"
She told me (that) she eats lunch at 1pm every day.

Direct speech: present continuous   Reported speech: past continuous

"*I'm working on it.*"   **He said he was working on it.**

56

Direct speech: past simple

"John ate a sandwich for lunch."

Reported speech: past perfect

She said John had eaten a sandwich.

Direct speech: past continuous

"We were watching a movie."

Reported speech: past perfect continuous

They told me (that) they had been watching a movie.

Direct speech: present perfect

"I have traveled to 10 countries."

Reported speech: past perfect

He told me he had traveled to 10 countries.

Direct speech: past perfect

"I had finished the test right before the bell rang."

Reported speech: past perfect (no change)

He said (that) he had finished the test right before the bell rang.

Say/said doesn't have an indirect object but **tell/told** must have an indirect object

He said he was tired.

*He told **me** he was tired.*

When reporting speech you can include or omit 'that'.

> He said **that** he was tired. / He said he was tired. (Both okay)
>
> He told me **that** he was tired. / He told me he was tired. (Both okay)

Requests, orders, and **advice** can be reported using an infinitive instead of changing the tense of the verb. We usually use ask, tell, and advise to report requests, orders, and advice.

> "Could you hold this for a moment?"
>
> He **asked me** to hold this for a moment.

> "You should get more sleep."
>
> The doctor **advised me** to get more sleep.

> "Take out a pencil and paper."
>
> The teacher **told us** to take out a pencil and paper

Modals also change:

Direct – Reported Speech

will - would

may - might

must – had to

can – could

But some modals don't change:

Direct – Reported Speech

should – should

would – would

could – could

When reporting **questions**, say or tell cannot be used. **Ask** is usually used, although **wonder** and **want to know** can also be used.

"Where are you from?"

*She **asked me** where I was from.*

"Where is he going?"

*Amy **wondered** where he was going. / Amy **wanted to know** where he was going.*

Reported speech questions

- What's some advice your parents told you?

- What did one of your teachers always tell you to do?

- What was the last question someone asked you?

- What's something strange someone said to you recently?

- What was the last time someone asked you to do something? What did they ask?

- What did you parents always tell you to do?

- What was a great piece of advice that someone gave to you?

- When was the last time someone asked you for money? What did they say?

- What's something you always tell people about yourself?

- Has anyone told you an interesting piece of news recently? What did they tell you?

- What did the last homeless person you met say to you?

- What's some advice you gave a friend recently?

- What was a surprising question that someone asked you?

- What's a memorable quote from someone you look up to?

- What did your parents always tell you not to do?

- What do you say to telemarketers when they call?

- What was the last thing you said to your friend?

SIMPLE PAST

To form the **simple past**, add –**ed** to the verb for regular verbs in affirmative sentences.

We use the **simple past** to:

Talk about an action that was completed once in the past.

   *He **talked** to the CEO yesterday.*

Talk about an action that was completed multiple times in the past.

   *She **walked** to school every day for a month.* (She doesn't walk to school anymore.)

Talk about something that was true for some time in the past but isn't true now.

   *We **worked** together in the same office.* (They don't work in the same office anymore.)

Use **did** to form questions and **did + not** (**didn't**) to form negatives. When **did** is used in a sentence it shows the past tense so the verb stays in its base form.

   *He **worked**.*

   *Where **did** he **work**?*

   ***Did** he **work**?*

   *He **didn't work**.*

There are **irregular verbs**. Unlike regular verbs, irregular verbs change form unpredictably and need to be memorized.

> *They **ate**.*
>
> *What **did** they **eat**?*
>
> *They **ate** steak.*
>
> ***Did** they **drink** wine?*
>
> *No, they **drank** water.*

When using the past tense form of the *be*-verb there are some exceptions. The verb changes form depending on the subject (**was/were**). **Did** isn't necessary with the *be*-verb to make questions or the negative.

> *I **was** tired. / Amy **was** tired. / We **were** tired. / You **were** tired.*
>
> *Where **was** the suitcase? / Where **were** the suitcases?*
>
> ***Was** the shirt blue? / **Were** the shirts blue?*
>
> *He **wasn't** there. / You **weren't** there.*

Simple past questions

- What did you do yesterday?

- Where did you go on your last vacation?

- What was the last restaurant you went to? How was it?

- What did you do last weekend?

- What did you eat for lunch yesterday?

- What was the last movie you saw? How was it?

- Who did you hang out with last? What did you do together?

- Talk about the last time you were surprised by something.

- What was the last game you played?

- When was the last time you rode a bicycle?

- Were you a well behaved child? Explain.

- What was a funny movie you watched recently?

- Talk about a time you were lost.

- Where did you grow up? What was it like?

- What was the last book you read?

- What did you do this morning?

- Tell me about the last time you were really excited.

SIMPLE PRESENT

The **simple present** is formed with the **base form** of the main verb. However, an agreement 's' (*He works.* / *They work.*) must be added to the main verb if the subject is third person singular (*he, she, it, John, the car*). When the main verb links the subject to an adjective, we use am, are, or is, depending on the subject.

I like music. / He likes music.

I am happy. / You are happy. / She is happy.

The car is blue. / The cars are blue.

When making negative sentences use **doesn't / don't,** or in the case of the *be*-verb use **isn't / aren't.**

When making questions use **do / does,** or in the case of the *be*-verb use **is / are.** (An exception being most 'who' questions).

She is tired. They are worried.

He doesn't like apples. I don't play the piano.

He is happy. The earth isn't flat.

When does he wake up?

Does she exercise every day?

Is the restaurant near here?

Who lives next door to you?

We use the **simple present** to:

Talk about something that is true in the present.

*I **am** an accountant.*

Talk about things that are always true.

*The earth **orbits** the sun.*

Talk about repeated actions or habits.

*He **brushes** his teeth every day.*

Talk about events in the near future that have a fixed time.

*The movie **starts** at nine.*

Adverbs of frequency are often used with the present tense to explain how often a repeated action or habit happens.

*She **sometimes plays** basketball.*

Simple present questions

- What do you do to get rid of stress?

- What do you eat or drink when it is really hot outside?

- What TV shows do you watch regularly?

- Where do you usually eat lunch?

- What do you do if you are bored?

- Who do you hang out with most?

- What app do you use the most?

- When do you usually wake up?

- Who do you talk to when you have problems?

- Do you prefer meat or fresh vegetables?

- When you're on vacation, do you relax or try to do many things?

- What do you do if you need to learn about something?

- Do you like to try new things? Why or why not?

- What are some hobbies you have?

- When do you buy a new phone? (i.e. when a new phone comes out, your phone breaks, etc.)

- What do you do to help yourself fall asleep?

- Do you dance when no one is watching? When do you dance?

SUPERLATIVES

Superlatives are used to compare a person or thing with every other person or thing in the same group.

For 1 syllable adjectives: **the + adjective –est**

*He is **the tallest** member of his family.*

For 2 or more syllable adjectives: **the + most + adjective** (to show the opposite use **least** instead of **most** before the adjective)

*This ring is **the most expensive** ring in the store.*

For adjectives ending in y: **drop the y** and use **the + adjective –iest**

*She is **the funniest** person here.*

There are exceptions – **good (best), bad (worst), far (furthest/farthest)**, etc.

Superlative questions

- What's the largest structure you've ever seen?

- What's the most delicious meal you've ever eaten?

- What's the most amazing hotel you've stayed at?

- Who is your best friend? Why are they your best friend?

- What's the worst recent movie?

- What's the most exciting thing you've ever done?

- What's the most popular tourist attraction in your country?

- What's the saddest book you've ever read?

- What's the most inspirational book you've ever read?

- Where is the best place to go to think?

- When was the most exciting period of your life?

- Who is the happiest person you know?

- What's the most addictive game you've ever played?

- Where is the worst place in your country to live? How about the best place to live?

- What's the greatest TV series you've watched?

- What's the weirdest movie you have ever seen?

- What's the strangest restaurant or bar you've been to?

TAG QUESTIONS

Tag questions are short questions at the end of sentences and are used to confirm information in the main part of the sentence or ask for agreement with the main part of the sentence.

Tag questions are most often used in spoken English.

We put a comma before the tag question.

If the **main part of the sentence is positive**, the **tag question is negative**.

> *You're hungry, **aren't you?***
>
> *John texted you, **didn't he?***

If the **main part of the sentence is negative**, the **tag question is affirmative**.

> *You're not hungry, **are you?***
>
> *John didn't text you, **did he?***

If the main sentence uses an auxiliary verb (**be, have, do**) or a modal verb (**should, could, will,** etc.) the same auxiliary verb or modal verb is used in the tag question.

> *Amy **is** going to be late, **isn't** she?*
>
> *We **shouldn't** go in there, **should** we?*

If the main sentence doesn't use an auxiliary verb or modal verb, then we use **do** for the tag question.

*They painted the house, **didn't they?***

*He walks to school, **doesn't he?***

We use the **same tense** for the main part of the sentence and the tag question.

If we really want to know the answer to a tag question, we put **rising intonation** on the tag question.

If we are looking for agreement, we put **falling intonation** on the tag question.

To **answer tag questions**, don't worry about whether the tag question is negative or affirmative. Just answer the **base question**.

> *You're hungry, **aren't you?** – Are you hungry? – **Yes, I am.***
>
> *You aren't hungry, **are you?** – Are you hungry? – **Yes, I am.***

The answer stays the same whether the tag question is negative or affirmative.

Tag question conversation questions

- You have a job, don't you?

- You've been abroad, haven't you?

- You haven't been to Disney World, have you?

- You can speak three languages, can't you?

- You're not going to work this weekend, are you?

- You'll go on vacation soon, won't you?

- You don't like pizza, do you?

- You haven't been to Mongolia, have you?

- You play a lot of mobile games, don't you?

- You got enough sleep last night, didn't you?

- You're going to see a movie this weekend, aren't you?

- You're not tired today, are you?

- Your birthday isn't this month, is it?

- You don't like cats, do you?

- You've eaten insects before, haven't you?

- You play football, don't you?

- You can't play basketball, can you?

USED TO, WOULD

Used to and **would** are both used to talk about the past. We use **used to** and **would** to talk about things that started in the past and finished in the past.

Used to is used to talk about past states or repeated actions in the past. **Did** or **didn't** show past tense so if they are used, **used to** becomes **use to**.

> *I didn't **use to** live in an apartment.* (past state)
>
> *He **used to** take the train to work every day.* (repeated action)
>
> *Did she **use to** play video games in the afternoon?* (repeated action)

Would is only used to talk about repeated actions in the past.

> *My friends **would** bring their lunch to school.* (repeated action)

So we can use **used to** and **would** interchangeably if they are being used to talk about repeated actions.

> *He **used to** take the train to work every day.*
>
> *He **would** take the train to work every day.*

> *Did she **use to** play video games all afternoon when she was younger?*
>
> ***Would** she play video games all afternoon when she was younger?*

> *My friends **used to** bring their lunch to school.*
>
> *My friends **would** bring their lunch to school.*

But we can only use **used to** to talk about states in the past.

*I didn't **use to** live in an apartment.* (used to, not would)

If an action happens only once in the past the **past simple** is used rather than **used to** or **would**.

Used to, would questions

- What would you do for fun when you were a child?

- What games did you use to play when you were young?

- Who would help you with your homework when you were in junior high school?

- Did you use to get into a lot of trouble when you were a kid? Why or why not?

- Whose house would you go to when you were in elementary school?

- What snacks did you use to eat all the time but now dislike?

- What restaurant would your family go to a lot when you were a child? Do they still go there?

- Are there any embarrassing fashion trends you used follow?

- Who did you use to play with in elementary school?

- What would you usually do after school finished when you were younger?

- Did you use to build forts when you were a child?

- Where would you hangout when you were a teenager?

- What used to be your favorite toy?

- What extracurricular activities did you use to do?

- How would you get home from elementary school?

- What are some things people used to do in your country but don't now?

- What game did you use to play a lot when you were younger?

WILL

We use the modal verb **will + main verb** to talk about the future. Modals are used by the speaker/writer to indicate their feelings about the proposition that they are making. When using the modal **will**, they are expressing intentionality or certainty. In speech and informal writing **will** is often shortened to 'll for affirmative or **won't** for negative

We use **will** to:

Make predictions or express certainty about the future.

> *Humans **will land** on the moon again in the next 10 years.*
>
> *The sun **will rise** tomorrow.*

Make offers or suggestions.

> *I'**ll help** you with your bags.*
>
> *He'**ll get** that for you.*

Make promises, requests, warnings, or threats.

> *We'**ll help** you paint your house.*
>
> *Do your homework or you'**ll get** a bad grade in the class.*

Talk about a decision made spontaneously at the time of speaking.

> *Oh no, the car is almost out of gas. I'**ll stop** here and fill up.*

Talk about what people want to do or are willing to do.

*Will you **help** him with his math homework?*

*Sure I'll **help** him.*

The following questions focus more on the use of will to make predictions about the future. This is because most books focus specifically on this use of will.

Will questions

- What will your life be like in 5 years?

- How will communication change in the future?

- What do you think the world will look like in 50 years?

- Will you ever go sky diving? Why or why not?

- How will entertainment change in the future?

- What will transportation look like in the future?

- What will you do when you retire?

- Will robots become part of daily life in the future? Why or why not?

- Will the future be better or worse than the present? Why or why not?

- What will video games be like in 7 years?

- What will happen to privacy in the future?

- Will alternative energy technologies solve the world's energy problems? Why or why not?

- Where will humans explore next?

- What will have the biggest impact on you in the near future?

- Will humans ever colonize another solar system? Why or why not?

- What company will change society the most? Will it be a good change or bad change?

- Will the borders of countries be more open or more closed in the future?

- What will happen if the world's population keeps increasing at its current rate?

WOULD RATHER, PREFER

We use **would rather** and **(would) prefer** to talk about general preferences and specific preferences. They can be used interchangeably. **Prefer** can be used with or without 'would'.

When we are talking about **general preferences**:

Prefer is followed by **verb-ing**.

> *I prefer hiking.*

Would rather is followed by the **bare infinitive** (just the verb).

> *I would rather read.*

When we are comparing general preferences we use **to** with **prefer** and **than** with **would rather**.

> *I prefer hiking to swimming.*

> *I would rather read than watch a movie.*

When we are talking about **specific preferences**:

Prefer is followed by **to + infinitive** (to + verb).

> *I prefer to eat pizza tonight.*

Would rather is followed by the **bare infinitive** (just the verb).

I would rather take a taxi after we eat.

When we are comparing specific preferences we use **rather than** with **prefer** and **than** with **would rather.**

*I prefer to eat pizza **rather than** seafood tonight.*

*I would rather take a taxi **than** a bus after we eat.*

Would rather, prefer questions

- Would you rather be very beautiful/handsome and poor, or very ugly and rich? Why?

- Would you rather be great at painting or programming? Why?

- Do you prefer to eat at home or eat at a restaurant? Why?

- Would you rather go to the beach or go to the mountains while on vacation? Why?

- Do you prefer living in a city or living in the countryside? Why?

- Which do you prefer, watching TV or reading books? Why?

- Would you rather go to a museum or go to a club? Why?

- Do you prefer hotels or hostels? Why?

- Would you rather own a cat or a dog? Why?

- Would you rather sail around the world or go into space? Why?

- Which do you prefer, outdoor work or house work? Why?

- Would you prefer to be very intelligent or very clever? Why?

- Would you rather own a sports team or a popular restaurant? Why?

- Do you prefer going out to parties or enjoying quiet nights at home? Why?

- Do you prefer traveling in a tour group or traveling alone? Why?

- Would you rather go someplace you know is good or a new place that might be good? Why?

- Would you rather save the lives of five people you don't know or save the life of one person you do know?

USING CONVERSATION QUESTIONS IN THE CLASSROOM

Let me begin by saying, these tips on how to use conversation questions in the classroom are based on what I have found to work in my classes. You may have to tweak or disregard some of my advice to accommodate your own teaching style. With that in mind, let's get started.

Timing

First, let's talk about how much time to allocate for questions. When planning lessons, I most often follow a rough rule of a minimum of one minute per question and a maximum of three minutes per question. That doesn't really indicate how much time they will spend on each individual question; it's just a rough estimate for judging the amount of time it will take to finish a set of questions.

So if you give your students ten questions, you'll burn between ten to thirty minutes of class time. Now of course this isn't a steadfast rule. There will always be exceptions. All things considered though, about twenty minutes for ten questions is the average for my classes.

Another quick point, if you can limit how many questions they see at a time (using PowerPoint or spaced handouts) they will answer questions more fully and take more time. I find showing them five questions at a time makes for a good pace.

Group Size

Next, you need to decide how many students to put into each group. As a general rule of thumb I find that three students in a group is the ideal number. I say this because with three students everyone gets a good chance to talk but there are still enough people to have a rich reservoir of ideas to discuss.

Two students really maximize talking time, but often the two students don't get along or you might have two shy students that end up together.

Four students can work, but often there isn't enough talk time for each student and shy students feel like they are on stage every time they talk.

Five students in a group is far too many and often they just won't talk. All this being said, ultimately it comes down to the dynamics of your class and its size.

If you have a really talkative class with a good dynamic, putting them in pairs works well. Groups of four generally work best with groups of shy students, because they feel more pressure to speak if everyone in the group is silent.

Mistakes are okay

Assure your students that mistakes are okay. Tell them they should try to produce the target grammar correctly. If they make mistakes unrelated to the target grammar, let them know that it's okay. Tell them that you are happy when they make mistakes because that means they are trying new and difficult ways of saying things.

One thing to stress is that they shouldn't be speaking their native language. It is better to say something that is incorrect or unclear in English than correctly and clearly in their first language.

Let the conversation flow

Another important point to stress is that they are free to discuss more than just the questions. Even though you are trying to focus on practicing grammar, a natural conversation moves from one subject to another; and this is what you want in your classes as well. As long as they are practicing the target grammar most of the time, don't get involved.

Very often students will treat questions like an ordered set of goals to accomplish. Let them know if they don't discuss them all, that's okay!

If they spend the whole time talking about just one question, that's great. It means they are having a natural conversation. Just make sure they are speaking only in English! I tell my students they can discuss whatever questions they think are interesting. If they don't think any questions are interesting, they should make their own questions.

Keep out of the discussion

After you have put the students into groups and they are talking, there is one important point to remember. Stay out of the discussion! I know it may be tempting to make a comment, but this is their time to discuss.

The only time you should be interrupting their discussion is when they ask you for help. Sometimes you can interject if a student is repeatedly using the target grammar incorrectly. You don't want them practicing the grammar point incorrectly. Otherwise, stay out of the discussion.

So what are you doing while they are discussing? You are monitoring each group's discussion and taking notes.

Take notes

While you are monitoring your students' discussions, you should be taking notes. Take note of any errors that are being made repeatedly (i.e. errors in grammar, pronunciation or vocabulary use), especially problems with the target grammar. Write down some specific sentences that contain common errors you hear or that contain errors you wish to work on.

Decide which errors or mistakes would be useful to go over with the class and at the end of class or at the end of the discussion go over some of these mistakes and errors. When you go over the errors, keep them anonymous and let students know that it's a good thing if they see their mistake on the board. You might let the class try to correct the errors or correct them yourself for the class depending on how much time you have.

So those are the tips I have for using conversation questions in an adult ESL class. You may find that these tips don't suit your teaching style. Give them a try and if they don't mesh with your teaching style, try something different. Every teacher teaches differently and every student learns differently. Ultimately the goal is to find what works best for you and your class.

JOIN OUR REVIEWER PROGRAM

We are always looking for qualified reviewers for our books. But we don't want to offer free review copies to just anyone. We want to offer them to people who are more likely to leave a review since they have left reviews in the past.

So if you leave a review of this book and are interested in receiving a free digital copy of one of our books as a review copy, let me know which of the reviews is yours and which book you are interested in at:

larrypitts@eslconversationquestions.com

We only ask that you actually review the review copy we send you. Once you write a review of the book we sent you, we can send you a digital review copy of another one of our books.

We'll also send you a review copy of any new books we come out with.

ENJOY THE BOOK?

Check out our other books

You can find the PDFs for our other books on our website (eslconversationquestions.com) or paperback and Kindle versions on Amazon. You can also ask your local book store if they carry our books.

ESL Role Plays: 50 Engaging Role Plays for ESL and EFL Classes

1,000 Conversation Questions: Designed for Use in the ESL or EFL Classroom

ESL Worksheets and Activities for Kids

IELTS Study Guide: Quick Tips, Tricks, and Strategies

Or why not leave a review on Amazon?

Every review makes a big difference. Reviews help other teachers find our books on Amazon. So if you think this book can help others, let them know on Amazon. I really appreciate it!

Plus if you leave a review, you can join our review club and get free review copies of our new books and other books in our growing collection. You can find out more on the previous page.

Questions, suggestions, or problems?

I love hearing feedback from readers. If you have any questions I would be happy to answer them. If you have suggestions for this book or a suggestion for a new book I would love to hear about them.

Also, if you have any problems or if you noticed any mistakes I would love to hear about them so I can fix them.

You can reach me by email: **larrypitts@eslconversationquestions.com**